Football

Funerals

Clubs

Cops

Après la Guerre

Playing the Pokies

Telephoning

Picnicking

Hospital Visiting

Introductions

AUSSIE ETIKET
or
Doing Things the Aussie Way

Also by John O'Grady
(Combined sales exceed one million copies)

They're A Weird Mob
Cop This Lot
No Kava For Johnny
Gone Fishin'
The Things They Do To You
Aussie English
Gone Troppo
O'Grady Sez
So, Sue Me!

AUSSIE ETIKET

or

Doing Things the Aussie Way

JOHN O'GRADY

Illustrated by Benier

URE SMITH · SYDNEY

First published in Australia 1971
by Ure Smith, Sydney
155 Miller Street, North Sydney 2060
a division of Horwitz Group Books
2 Denison Street, North Sydney 2060

Copyright © John O'Grady, 1971

Second impression October 1971

National Library of Australia Card
Number and ISBN 0 7254 0067 6

Designed and produced in Australia
Printed in Australia at The Griffin
Press, Adelaide

Registered in Australia for transmission
by post as a book

CONTENTS

	Introduction	1
1.	Afternoon Tea	4
2.	Après la Guerre	7
3.	Barbecues	11
4.	Christenings	13
5.	Clubs	16
6.	Cops	18
7.	Correspondence	21
8.	Dining Out	24
9.	Dress	26
10.	Fishing	28
11.	Football	32
12.	Funerals	36
13.	Golf	38
14.	Hospital Visiting	41
15.	Introductions	47
16.	Loving Thy Neighbour	49
17.	Motoring	54
18.	Picnicking	58
19.	Pie Eating	60
20.	Playing the Pokies	62
21.	Pubs	64
22.	Speech Making	68
23.	Telephoning	71
24.	Transport	76
25.	Weddings	81
26.	Wine Tasting	84

Introduction

'Etiquette' is a French word, adopted by the English in those remote times when French was the language of diplomacy and politeness. 'Rendezvous' and 'RSVP' survive from the same snobbish social period.

My dictionary defines 'etiquette' as 'The forms required by good breeding, or prescribed by authority, to be observed in social or official life; observance of the proprieties of rank and occasion; conventional decorum.'

It was 'observed' mainly by the upper classes, such as earls and other kinds of 'noblemen in the counties', one of whom is mentioned on labels of Holbrook's sauce bottles.

These people were called 'parfait gentil hommes', later to become known as 'perfect gentlemen'.

When observing a knight in shining armour riding a lolloping, splay-footed draught horse across your best malting barley patch, 'conventional decorum' demanded that you greeted him with, 'Avaunt there, sirrah. Comest thou in peace?' If he said, 'Nay, sirrah, cometh I to joust with thee,' then you were required to pull off your glove – gloves were worn by all perfect gentlemen to hide their dirty fingernails – and stroke him lightly across the visor with it.

A true gentleman would never say, 'Get outa there you useless big bastard an' stop trampin' down my barley, or I'll lop yer lolly off.' Such language was considered to be vulgar – vulgar meaning 'pertaining to people' – and was only used when talking to people.

The lower classes were known as 'people'. They owned no horses, no suits of shining armour, and in the opinion of gentlemen were fit only to cultivate a gentleman's fields, or to get themselves killed in his wars.

Gentlemen's female consorts were called ladies – or mistresses – and were given fine raiment and jewellery in payment for their services. The female consorts of the lower classes were called women, and were given bread, when there was any about.

'The forms required by good breeding' were practised by well-bred ladies and gentlemen in their relations with each other.

Any family that inherited property, from ancestors who acquired it by murder, theft or dirty politics, or families who got some for themselves by such methods, were persons of good breeding. Those who owned nothing, and worked for a living, were ill bred, and the word 'etiquette' did not apply to them.

Catherine the Great of Russia, when told that the peasants were revolting, said, 'Yes, aren't they?'

Queen Marie Antoinette of France, when told that the people had no bread, said, 'Give them cake.'

King Edward the Seventh of England said, 'I don't care what the people do, as long as they don't do it in the streets and frighten the horses.'

And Governor Hunter said of the people of Australia, 'A more wicked, abandoned, and irreligious set of people have never been brought together in any part of the world.'

It will be seen that ladies and gentlemen of good breeding did not think much of people. And people, when European etiquette was first imported into Australia, certainly did not think much of gentlemen of good breeding. (Ladies in that category were scarce at the time.) And this was hardly fair, because gentlemen were never known to flog people. They always got one of the lower orders to do it.

This gentlemanly etiquette, now called 'delegation of authority', or 'passing the buck', still survives in our country. And in some minority circles, other etiquettes imported from France via England – '1066 and all that' – also survive. For example, gentlemen of good breeding, wearing olde English-style suits and ties, are sometimes seen opening car doors for their ladies – or mistresses.

Admittedly such 'observance of the proprieties' is rare – taxi drivers have long discarded it – but, like the practice of sending the ladies away from the dining-table while the gentlemen indulge themselves with tobacco, grog and dirty yarns, it does survive.

In general, however, Australians have little reverence for such relics of ancient gentlemanly behaviour patterns, and have developed their own social customs and graces. The purpose of this book is to describe and explain some of them – the more generally practised – so that visiting Englishmen and a few Americans may not be embarrassed. We are basically a very polite people, and would not willingly permit any visitor to feel uncomfortable through lack of knowledge of our 'conventional decorum'.

We will call this 'conventional decorum' 'etiket', since very few of us speak or understand French.

Afternoon Tea

In the stately homes of England, 'Tea' is served at four o'clock in the afternoon. It comes in a silver pot, and is poured into small cups made of thin and delicate china, and there are thin and delicate cucumber sandwiches on the side.

Not in Australia. Silver teapots were flogged to antique dealers years ago; thin and delicate china was broken in the washing up; and nobody would be seen dead within a hundred yards of a cucumber sandwich.

In the red-roofed homes of Australia, afternoon tea, if it is served at all, will be poured from an old brown pot with a 'cosy' on it, and you will sit 'at the table', and there will be fruit cake, and sponge cake, and lamingtons, and 'marangs', and ham sandwiches, and egg sandwiches, and hot buttered scones. And it will be Sunday afternoon.

You will do well to eat plenty, because if you are 'staying on for tea' – you will be asked – there will be nothing for 'tea' except the cold remains of the 'leg o' lamb' that the family had for dinner, and not much left to 'go around'.

If you are an American, don't say, 'May I have another soda biscuit, please?' The correct phrase is, 'Smack us in the kisser with another scone, will ya?'

Afternoon teas in Australian homes are for women and teetotallers. You will notice that your host leaves his chair frequently and goes away for a minute or two. You will be wrong if you think he has a weak bladder. He is going out to his garage. Follow him. That's where the grog will be.

'Ah,' he'll say. 'Same idea, eh? The only way a man can stand bloody afternoon tea is to have a couple or three slugs. Get that into you. Gees, those women c'n yap, can't they?'

Office workers, notably public servants, specialize in morning tea – coffee-break to you Americans – but afternoon tea is also known to them.

Real workers, who use their hard and horny hands, and the muscles of their shoulders, backs and legs, call such pauses for refreshment 'smoko'. The billy – a battered and blackened old container with a wire handle on it, or on big jobs a four-gallon kero-tin in similar condition – is filled with water and boiled by the Peggy. He's usually an unskilled labourer, generally regarded as 'bloody useless' if he has to be *told* to 'go an' put the billy on.'

On the Peggy's call of 'Smoko' all tools are dropped, and work ceases for an official ten minutes, which is normally extended to twenty, and sometimes thirty, depending on the subject under discussion.

'Gawd strike me bloody dead – look what me missus's given me for smoko. Skinny bloody sliced bread, an' peanut bloody butter.'

'Aw, feed it to the currawongs, mate. Have one o' mine. Curried egg. Inch-an'-a-half thick.'

'I got a hunk o' cake here. Too much for me. Half of it interest you?'

Food, provided by wives for smoko and lunch, and shared with mates or thrown to the birds, is always good as a subject for a twenty-minute discussion. But as a theme, thrown in as a statement, and opposed and defended, no subject is more popular than 'The boss is a bastard.' It's always good for thirty minutes. And if it starts at three o'clock and finishes about three-thirty, then it's too late to 'saddle up' again, because the job has to be cleaned up, and the gear collected and stowed in time for the official 'knock off' at four-thirty – normally about four.

The best and most interesting kind of 'tea' is 'smoko'.

Après la Guerre

He was a young American from Chicago, via South Vietnam. He was lean and clean and crew cut, and he was telling us about his experiences up there. Conditions were really rugged, he said. Charlie was unpredictable and vicious.

Addo asked him, 'Who's Charlie?'

'VC,' he said.

'Oh well, I s'pose you have to be unpredictable and vicious to get a VC.'

Peto said, 'VC means Viet Cong, you mug. Septic Tanks don't get VCs. They get purple hearts.'

'Oh,' Addo said. 'Must be all that ice-cream they eat. Sends their blood pressure up.'

The young bloke said that where he was stationed they didn't get much ice-cream. And nearly every night they got mortared.

Addo said, 'Peto just gets bombed.'

Peto ignored this slander, and the young American looked puzzled.

Addo said, 'Anyway, what are you doing down here?'

'I came down on R an' R,' the Yank said.

'Never heard of it, mate. Is it a ship or a 'plane?'

'R an' R,' Peto said, 'means rest and recuperation.'

Addo said, 'From what?'

'From the horrors of war.'

'Oh. You mean not enough ice-cream?'

'Could be,' Peto said. 'I remember in New Guinea in '42, we didn't get any ice-cream for a fortnight. We were real upset.'

'I believe New Guinea was pretty rugged, too,' the Yank said.

'Yeah,' Addo said. 'Once, on the old Kokoda Track, we didn't get any soap powder for a week.'

'Heard about that,' Peto said. 'But that was the ASC right through. You were in the Western Desert as well, weren't you?'

'Was I in the Western Desert? Now look, Montgomery says to me . . .'

'I know what he said to you. He said, "That man there. You, soldier. Good God man, that is not the purpose for which the tin hat was invented." '

'Oh well,' Addo said. 'I'm just naturally modest.'

The Yank asked, 'What's a tin hat?'

'Now you take soap,' Peto said, ignoring him and sticking to the subject. 'I'll admit they did a good job with the water. I mean a pint of water per man per day for drinking, shaving and bathing, is plenty, when it's only a hundred an' twenty in the shade. But every day we got a cake of Cashmere Bouquet soap. And if there's one brand of soap I can't stand, it's Cashmere Bouquet.'

'Yeah. Same thing happened to us with tomato sauce. For a whole month we're getting steak an' eggs for breakfast, an' all they've got's Rosella tomato sauce. No PMU. No Rich Red Fountain. Just Rosella.'

'I remember that. But it wasn't the tomato sauce I was crooked on. It was steak an' eggs every day, when a man's dying for a decent feed of M an' V, or Goldfish.'

'Or egg powder. Now you weren't with us that time we were up in Kukukuku country in New Guinea, were you?'

'No, I missed out on that.'

'Mate, you were lucky. We only got clean sheets every third day. Only every third day. In the Tropics. I mean, sheets get sweaty in the Tropics.'

'Tough. Where I was, around Wau, we were all right for sheets. But the beer. Now, a man goes out on patrol. A fighting patrol. You know what that means. When a man's risking his life he deserves some amenities, right?'

'Right.'

'So we've got these blokes in the middle with the eskies an' the ice, an' it comes smoko time. An' you know what they've got? Bulimba Gold Top. Nothing else. Every esky full of Bulimba Gold Top.'

'Gee, mate, I didn't know you were with that mob. It wasn't always the ASC though. The top brass did some shocking things to us. Remember that time they decided we needed some R an' R, an' they flew us back to Australia for a week with our wives?'

'Yeah. In a fleet of Catalinas. Couldn't stand those Cats. Too slow an' noisy.'

'Where did your mob go?'

'Brisbane.'

'We – believe it or not – we were flown to Melbourne, an' had to stay at Young an' Jackson's, lookin' at Chloe all the time. An' the whole town full of Septic Tanks eatin' all the bloody ice-cream.'

The young American said, 'My father was down here in Australia during World War Two.'

'Was he?' Peto said. 'Did he get a purple heart?'

'He got one some place.'

'Probably some Nine Div bloke shot him,' Addo said.

'You know,' the Yank said, 'I think you two are putting me on.'

'Don't know what that means, mate. But whatever it is, we wouldn't dream of it, would we?'

And Peto said, 'No. We're just applying a little traction to the pedal extremities.'

Serious-minded young visitors, with recent memories of modern warfare, should beware of this type of Aussie conversational etiket. It is practised extensively by old soldiers. And Air Force types. And Navy bods.

Barbecues

Barbecues, on fine Saturdays or Sundays, are a feature of the Australian suburban and country landscape. That haze that you see covering the continent as you fly in is not fog. It is chop-sausage- and steak-flavoured wood or charcoal smoke which will delight your nose when you descend from the aircraft.

Anti-pollution laws do not, and probably never will, apply to barbecues.

When you have made friends with a few of the indigenous inhabitants of our country, you will be invited to a barbecue. The etiket:

Dress: Extremely casual. Never, never, never suit and tie.

Gifts: An attractive and interesting female will be welcome, since there is no sex segregation at barbecues. But an off-white butcher's paper parcel of cookable meats will insult your host. He will always 'know a butcher' who gives him the 'best cuts', and he will have 'laid on' enough for everybody. If you feel that you must bring something in lieu of, or in addition to an interesting and attractive female, bring half-a-dozen of beer, or a flagon of Red Ned.

(Red Ned? 'Vin rouge ordinaire', officially labelled claret or dry red.)

Conventional Decorum: Women prepare the salads and all other trimmings, organize the plates, cutlery, glasses, condiments, etc (your bird's offer to help will be appreciated) and your host cooks the meats. He will be, by his own admission, the best barbecuer of steak, chops and sausages 'this side of the black stump'. And even if his chops are burnt, and his steaks ooze blood, and his sausages burst open at both ends, you *must* congratulate him and eat everything he puts on your plate. The words 'bloody good tucker, this' will be appropriate.

You must also register a favourable reaction to his humorous apron and his funny hat. But – and this is important – you must watch your language. The word 'bloody' is all right, but avoid all profanity unless and until your host gives you a lead. He may, when the women are washing up – your offer to help will 'get you in good' with the women, but will be politely refused – entertain you with a scurrilous song or two of Army, Navy or Air Force origin. In which case any contribution you may be able to make will 'get you in good' with him.

Finally, do not be either the first or the last to leave. A too early departure will reflect unfavourably on the quality of the hospitality, and an unduly delayed one may bring you a sarcastic offer of 'a bed for the night'. Go with the 'strength', and do not neglect to thank your hostess with a few appropriate words and a kiss on the cheek or hand. This will 'go down big', and ensure you another invitation.

Christenings

Most Australians are Christians of some sort or another and have their kids baptized, or 'christened'. These functions take place in a church, and are followed by an adjournment to the home of the parents, where afternoon tea – with or without grog, depending upon the parents' denomination, but mostly with – is served.

You could be present as a guest, in which case normal social etiket applies. That is, you talk to people, and enjoy the refreshments provided. You 'wet the baby's head'.

But you may be asked to be godfather, which means that should the parents become alcoholics, incapacitated, incapable, or dead, you will have the duty of caring for and educating the child, and guiding him or her on his or her merry little way through young life to the trials and troubles of adulthood. After which you can thankfully brush him or her off your hands.

It is a big responsibility, and could cost you, but it is not good etiket to refuse. When asked, you should say, 'Aw, beauty, mate. I'm honoured. If you get skittled, I'll look after the little bugger.' And you keep your fingers crossed, and go along to the church, and 'go through the performance'.

The etiket of the performance is probably best illustrated by the following true story, told to the author of this book of perfect behaviour by a friend who is a man of soul, generosity, kindness and courage, and who is very fond of kids, and other small animals.

He said, 'Sorry I wasn't home yesterday when you called in, mate. I was at a christenin'. Bloody godfather.'

'Oh? Who was christened?'

'Steve's little bloke – young Steve. You know Steve, the mate I work with?'

'Oh yes. But wasn't his kid born over a year ago?'

'Yeah. He's over a year old. They were a bit late wettin' his head. Gees, that kid caused me a lot o' trouble.'

'How come?'

'You know that path I put around me garden up the backyard?'

'Yes.'

'Well, before he was born, I was just startin' it. I had her dug out, and some forming up, and Steve comes to me an' says his missus is about ready to go off, an' would I keep an eye on her in case she had to go while he was at work. I was off on compo then, see, with me crook foot. She was good enough to hobble around on, but, long as I took me time. I'm mixin' on the floor of me garage with a shovel. I've got a seven-bucket mix down, all nice and wet and turned over, when I get a signal from Steve's missus. She's gotta go. She'd rung her doctor, an' he says straight to the hospital, no muckin' about. Well, I reckon I can get her there before me mix goes off, so I bung her into the car, an' off we go. When we get there they tell me to wait in case it's a false alarm. It was. I waited all the bloody afternoon, and just on dark Steve turns up an' takes over. By the time I get home me mix has gone right off, and I had to dig it off me garage floor with a mattock. Useless it was. Now you wouldn't read about this, but four days later I've got another mix down, just before lunch, nicely wet and turned over, an' she does it again. Gotta go in right away. I said a few words, but I took her in, an' you know what? They asked me to wait. I waited hours till Steve got there, then I came home an' started whackin' into me mix again with the mattock. Me garage floor's never been the same since. All lumpy, she is. Anyway, that second time was fair dinkum, an' she had young Steve.'

'And now you're his godfather.'

'Yeah. Had to hold the squirmin' little bugger all through the performance. There's a bit of a mob there, an' we had to wait, all the kids yowlin' except Steve's little bloke. First thing he does is knock the hat off an old chook sittin' in front of us. Then he pulls the hair of another one. By the time we front up to the sky pilot, I've had him. He's a long, skinny bloke, this sky pilot, with a fruity voice an' glasses. He says to me, "And what do you name this child?" I says, "Four Two One." He says, "I beg your pardon?" "Four Two One," I says. "Four o' metal, two o' sand, an' one o' cement." He won't be in it. Says it's not a suitable name. I says, "Well, how about Standard Mix?" He thinks about that, an' I reckon I would've got it through, but then Steve's missus butts in an' we had to christen him Steve. I reckon he would sooner've been called Four Two One or Standard Mix, because just as he's gettin' his head wet he lets fly with a beaut right cross an' knocks the sky pilot's glasses into the fountain.'

'So his name's Steve.'

'Yeah. Accordin' to his father an' mother. But I'm his godfather, an' that's higher than them. Far as I'm concerned his name's Four Two One. When he gets a bit bigger, I'm gunna give him a scutch hammer an' comb, an' he can clean the rest of himself off me garage floor."

Clubs

There are very few Australians who don't belong to a club of some sort, be it sporting or social, and most belong to clubs that own, rent, or are paying off their premises.

Inside these buildings, with their bars for drinking at, tables for eating at, kitchens for cooking in, toilets for the elimination of surplus drink and food, and space for various games of skill or chance, members seek refuge from work and home, and refreshment for mind and body.

(Service clubs, such as Rotary, Lions, Apex, VIEW etc, use other people's premises.)

With very few exceptions, clubs insist that members and their visitors conform to enforced rules of 'dress etiquette'. There appears to be no evidence that clubs have large investments in the rag trade, or the shoe leather business, but there are actually 'snooty clubs' whose managements insist that members and their guests wear ties and shoes at all times, and where shorts are forbidden, even when the thermometer goes over the ton.

One notable exception is the Arch McArthur Golf Club on South Molle Island, North Queensland, where you may see gentlemen playing golf in shorts only, their chests and feet bare, and entering the club house similarly unattired. Members of this club practise etiket at all times, both in dress and language.

Most golf clubs, however, expect their members to wear shirts and shoes; and bowling clubs require uniforms with hats; and they and others all expect their members to wear jackets and ties when dining.

Even RSL clubs, whose original members fought for the preservation of democracy and freedom, insist on conformity in matters of dress. Freedom of speech is encouraged, but freedom of feet is not.

Clubs are ruled by elected Directors or Management Committees. And it is well known that a camel is a horse designed by a committee.

Nevertheless, Australians love their clubs and like to 'sign visitors in'. So you will be invited.

Dress as for a wedding, or a funeral, and practise the etiquette of deportment and language. You may forget these last two when 'playing the pokies', but not the club's rules of dress.

Cops

Australian cops are well dressed, have excellent deportment, are very modest and unassuming, and have good manners. They are never abusive, are noted for their self-restraint, and may frequently be heard to call you 'sir'.

But they can be provoked, and when provoked they become excessively and unsmilingly polite, and ask you to 'accompany' them. This can cause you considerable inconvenience and delay, since you have no choice but to do as they ask. Therefore 'cop etiket', in your own interest, must be learnt.

The very best way to avoid being asked to 'accompany' a cop, or to 'come along to the station, sir', is to avoid the cop. But this cannot always be done, since sometimes cops will want to talk to you, and evasive tactics are then unwise. The safest rule is never to talk to a cop until he talks to you first.

You may think that when a cop on traffic duty beckons you through, it would be a kind friendly christian act to say, 'Thank you, Constable luv – I'll get the dear Sisters to say a little prayer for your dear old mother.'

It would not be a kind, friendly christian act. It would provoke him just as much as, 'Good morning, mug,' or 'May

I have the pleasure of the next dance?' Say nothing. Just nod your head if you want to please him. He will nod back and think to himself, 'Well well well – that's a nice gentleman.' Nods to cops are good public relations.

When a cop asks you a question, answer him politely and as briefly as possible. *Never* ask a question of your own such as, 'Who wants to know?' or 'What's it got to do with you, mug?' Such questions are not good public relations.

The only time you may ask a question is when you are driving along, minding your own business, and a uniform on a motorbike – or two uniforms in a car – come up alongside you and you hear the words, 'Pull over, driver.' (Cops never call drivers 'sir'.) At such a time, you pull over, and wait until a uniform approaches your window. Then you ask, 'What can I do for you, Sarge?'

It is good public relations to offer to help cops, and to give them higher rank than they actually possess. But if you meet one in a pub – he will, of course, be out of uniform – don't offer to buy him a drink, unless he buys you one first. Otherwise you could be called a 'crawler', or a 'brown nose', and these are not good things to be called.

When in trouble, 'call a cop', and you will receive help. But never call a cop a 'mug'. And as for the American epithet 'pig' – forget it and live. You can even be fined just for saying 'oink oink oink'.

A bloke we know named Ginger Neal was fined recently for making noises at a motorcycle cop.

'You wouldn't read about it,' he told us. 'Yesterday. Rainin' cats an' dogs, right?'

'Right.'

'I'm comin' along Henry Lawson Drive, visibility limited, wipers goin' flat out, an' bugger me if I don't get a flat tyre. No rain coat. Nothin'. Get out an' get soaking wet. Get the spare out o' the boot, get the jack out, an' start workin' an' swearin'. An' up comes this walloper on a motorbike. He pulls up an' says, "Having a bit of bad luck driver?" I says, "Yeah, mate." He says, "You'll get drowned there. I'll give you a hand." Well, I got no love for the wallopers, but fair dinkum, I reckoned that bloke was one of nature's gentlemen. He gives me a hand, an' puts the flatty an' the jack back in the boot for me, an' I says, "Thanks very much, mate." An' he says, "A pleasure, driver." An' then you know what the bastard did?'

'No. What?'

'Books me for puttin' a bald tyre on.'

'He didn't?'

'He did. Fair bloody dinkum. Books me.'

'That was a bit rough. The baldy would've got you home.'

'Course it would. Gees I was mad. I said a few words. Now I'm in more trouble.'

'How?'

'For the few words I said, that's how.'

'Oh? What'd you say?'

He told us. The few words cost him fifty dollars. Plus the fine for the bald tyre. Plus the price of a new one. He still doesn't like wallopers.

Uniformed cops are generally known as 'wallopers', and cops in plain clothes are called 'demons'. These latter, supposed to be disguised, are instantly recognizable. They are large, unsmiling men who walk slowly and wear hats.

There is another kind called 'brown bombers'. They are very interested in parked cars. They put chalk marks on tyres and leave little notes, in envelopes, under windscreen wipers. Their activities provoke car owners to describe them as a 'pack o' bastards', or to say, 'Gor strike, a bloody blister for a lousy extra ten minutes.'

Wallopers, demons and brown bombers, like the poor, 'are always with us'. They're only 'doin' their job', so it is good etiket to be kind to them.

Correspondence

68 Algernon Street
OATLEY NSW 2223
25 January, 1971

Messrs Throgmorton and McSwizzletossel
Solicitors
Umpteen William Street
MELBOURNE VIC 3000

Dear Sirs

Re: *Mullethead* v. *O'Grady*

Your communication AST/CL/186/71 of the 15th inst. refers.

It is the considered opinion of the writer that the action contemplated by you on behalf of your client can only result in an unnecessary disruption of an extremely congested Judicial schedule, and in a verdict unfavourable to your client, and with costs against him, accompanied by some pertinent comment from the Bench.

Your client's claim that his reputation has been damaged and his character assaulted by words used by the writer cannot be substantiated, due to lack of witnesses. He appears to have gained favour in your sight with a plausible story, as the reference in your communication to one hundred thousand dollars attests.

Without prejudice, the undersigned admits to having had an altercation with your client, but denies any liability in Law.

Yours faithfully,

John O'Grady

What a lot of codswallop. 'Messrs' indeed. Short for 'messieurs'. Very etiquette. And 'Dear Sirs'. We all know that solicitors are expensive, but is there any need to rub it in?

Or is 'Dear' a term of affection? If so, aren't we being a bit presumptuous calling strangers 'Dear'? How would we go if we started *a conversation* with a stranger by calling him 'Dear'? A man could finish up in hospital. Or in court, on a charge of making improper advances to a male.

And how about all that stilted phraseology in formal letters, with the first personal pronoun carefully avoided?

And that 'Yours faithfully'. Does that mean that we have surrendered our individuality, and now belong to somebody else, and promise to be faithful? Or is it just a bit of hypocritical bulldust?

As in conversation, the important things to remember in letter writing are to make your meaning clear, and to entertain the person on the receiving end – or at least not to be boring.

This is good etiket. As hereunder:

                                        68 Algernon Street
                                        OATLEY NSW 2223
                                        25-1-'71

Throgmorton & McSwizzletossel
Umpteen William Street
MELBOURNE 3000
Throggy —
You wrote to me ten days ago, and I've only just got your letter. Blame the PMG.

You're flogging a dead horse, mate, taking on that Mullet-head character. You'd have no show. I'll tell you what happened.

He was up here on holidays, having a few grogs on his Pat Malone, and I started to talk to him, because I felt sorry for him. But after a while he started to annoy me by skiting about Melbourne all the time, and I said, 'If it's such a great bloody place, why don't you piss off and go back to it?' Then he starts knocking Sydney, and one thing led to another, and I called him a 'prawn-headed mullet-gutted Victorian bastard', – amongst other things. But he can't sue me for that, because that's what he is. And in any case, we were in the gents at the time, and the only witnesses were the urinal and a couple of cisterns.

He hasn't got a leg to stand on, mate. Dump him. And you know what you can do with that claim for 100,000 bucks.

O'Grady

PS Don't do anything you couldn't do on a bike.

Now that's a good etiketical letter. The meaning is clear, the phraseology is not stilted and the PS is added for his entertainment.

The letters PS, by the way, stand for 'post scriptum'. Good etiket. Latin see. Not French.

Dining Out

There comes a time, in the life of every Australian family, when the Man of the House says, 'We're eatin' out tonight.' This rare statement could be motivated by a wedding anniversary, a birthday celebration, or an unexpected 'win at the races'.

The Man of the House will not be sober when he makes the statement. And before he can sober up and change his mind, which his wife's experience tells her he will do, she will fly around and organize the kids, including one of the neighbours as a baby-sitter if necessary, give herself a quick shower and a new face, and be dressed in minutes flat.

Australian wives love to be taken out to dinner, but are very rarely asked.

The Man of the House generally gets his generous brainwave while 'having a few grogs after work'. And that is where you come into the picture, because you will be having a few grogs with him and will be invited.

'Tell you what,' he'll say. 'We'll go home an' meet the missus, an' take her out to dinner.'

Now don't try to 'duck' this invitation, expressed as a statement. Go home with him and meet the missus. His offer to take her out to dinner is his way of 'squaring off' for having a few grogs and being late home, but you are his insurance and bait.

A well-dressed man, informal or casual, will stir her memories of the days when she was 'heart whole and fancy free', before she got tied up with the 'log' she married, and got 'saddled with a tribe of kids'. Instead of abusing her husband, she will greet you both with delight, and much batting of eyelashes and patting of hair, and apologies for the state of the house and the appearance of herself. Both of which she will alter very quickly.

You must remember to praise her home, her dress, and herself, because the Man of the House is 'squaring off', and your duty as a guest is to help him.

Whatever she wants, she is to be given – within reason. For example, if she wants to go 'to a decent restaurant for a change', this will be unreasonable. He will suggest the Chinese joint, and may compromise by agreeing to the Ities, or the Greeks. He may even eat Italian or Greek food washed down with Barossa Pearl, instead of 'steak an' eggs with trimmings' and a bottle of beer, which he would prefer. But a man must 'do the right thing by his missus' when he takes her out, even to the extent of ordering Chicken Maryland for her if she wants it.

A great many Australian women like Chicken Maryland.

You must 'do the right thing' by your host. Laugh at his stories. Order an exotic dish like Saltimbocca alla Romana to give him something to talk about. Be attentive to his lady. And suppress any temptation to discuss politics or religion.

In other words, when dining out, practise etiquette.

Dress

Australian dress customs are changing, and fairly rapidly. Any contribution you may be able to make towards improving the standard will be appreciated.

There was a time, not so long ago, when English gentlemen in Australia wore long underwear and fine linen, with heavy serge trousers and red jackets. Lower orders wore ankle chains, floppy Government issue suits with arrows on them, and on their backs the letters POHM. (Prisoner of His Majesty. Hence 'Pom', or 'Pommy'. One version, anyway.)

Native-born Australians then wore goanna grease, camp fire ashes, and clay. Even today very few of them wear that imported abomination called 'suit 'n tie'. You should assist in the campaign to have this form of dress condemned to death, like noxious weeds and vermin.

The following dress etiket is recommended:

Formal Summer Dress: Shirt, shorts, long socks and shoes. (If you have spindle shanks and knobby knees you may substitute slacks for shorts.)

Informal Summer Dress: Discard long socks and shoes in favour of thong sandals.

Casual Summer Dress: Discard thong sandals and shirt. (There are still some anachronistic and reactionary people, such as restaurant proprietors and fussy bar managers, who will not welcome you when attired in any one of the three forms of summer dress mentioned above. Etiket requires, with such people, that you say, 'Well, you know where to shove your bloody joint, mate', and that you go somewhere else.)

Winter Dress: On all winter occasions, formal, informal or casual, wear something – anything – to keep yourself warm.

Australia is divided laterally into three zones – temperate, sub-tropical, and tropical. But in some parts of the temperate zone, such as south of the Murray, a few months of winter may be experienced, and you may have to endure them.

If you do not have to endure them, then save clothing bills by going north.

Fishing

Fishing is a great Australian Sunday sport. It is practised mainly around the continental coastline where there is a plentiful supply of tidal rivers, creeks, inlets and lakes. Small boats are used, with or without small outboard motors.

After you have made friends you are sure to be invited to 'come fishin'' with us next Sunday'. In the meantime you can learn the etiket by observation.

Firstly, you will notice, it is necessary to do a 'pre-flight cockpit check'.

The boat will be tied up somewhere at a small landing, hanging on a line, with the tide trying to pull it free. There will be two men. One gets in and the other 'passes the gear'. Then the one in the boat gets out, and the two of them consume a couple of cans of lager.

The following conversation is then ritual – or perhaps we should say 'liturgy':

'Now listen, you silly mutt, in all that muckin' around, did you put the bait in?'

' 'Course I put the bloody bait in. D'yer think I'd go fishin' without bait?'

'Wouldn't surprise me. Remember the time you forgot beer?'

'That was *your* fault, an' well you know it.'
'Is the beer in?'
'Yes, the bloody beer's in. Two eskies.'
'Lines?'
'Wottayamean lines?'
'Fishin' bloody lines. They in?'
' 'Course they're in.'
'Hooks an' sinkers?'
'Yes.'
'Band-aids?'
'Yes.'
'Is the petrol can full? Last time we went out it was half empty.'
'Filled it meself this morning, while you were snorin' your head off.'
'Orright – tucker.'
'What about tucker? You're always thinkin' of your stomach. For your information, the tucker's in – corn beef sandwiches with mustard, chicken sandwiches, egg sandwiches, slabs of cake, an' some stale scones. Any complaints?'
'Yeah. I don't like mustard.'
'Well eat chicken an' egg. The tucker's in.'
'Well, all right. That's about the lot. Wotta we hangin' around here for? I'll get in, an' you untie the rope.'

He gets in. Number two casts off the line and throws it aboard. The boat takes off on the run-out tide.

'Hey, wait on,' he says. 'Come back. I'm not in yet.'
'I can see that,' says number one, fading downstream.

He quickly puts the rollocks in the gunnels and looks around for paddles, sculls and oars. There are none of these things in the boat. You will hear bursts of language floating back against the tide as he winds a cord around the outboard motor, and pulls. And pulls – and pulls. The motor refuses to start.

He throws out the kellick to anchor the boat against the

drift. The free end of the line has not been secured, and follows the kellick over the side. And the boat continues to drift downstream towards the ocean.

One hour later it is towed back by a half-cabin launch, whose owner wears a yachtsman's cap, and laughs all the time.

The boat is then tied up, and etiket demands that this operation be carried out in silence.

Only when the half-cabin launch with its laughing owner has steamed away is conversation resumed.

Number one says quietly, in a very polite tone, 'You would be the greatest bloody galah this side of the rabbit-proof fence. Where, may I ask, are the oars?'

Number two says, 'Where, may I ask, is the bloody kellick?'

Now safety precautions require that small boats should have both oars and a kellick, and the oars are many miles away in number two's garage, and the kellick is trailing its line twenty feet down amongst the silt and beer cans, being sniffed at by small bream.

'We'll fish here,' says number one, 'if you can remember not to untie the rope.'

And at the end of the day, with sunburnt knees and faces, and stomachs full of beer and sandwiches and cake and stale scones, they pack up and go home.

It is not good etiket to *buy* fish on the way home and display them proudly as your own catch. The correct behaviour is merely to state, 'She was a beaut day, but they were not biting.'

It is just possible, of course, that you may be invited out by professional fishermen, who work in the dark and cold of the night, and catch a lot of fish. In this case you must observe professional etiket, which is very simple, and can be summed up in one sentence – 'sit down, shut up, and keep quiet'.

Professional fishermen have no respect for amateur fishermen who dangle lines in daylight, on week-ends and public holidays, and whom professionals call 'anglers'. Anglers have no respect for professionals.

'Bloody river (or lake),' they say, 'is all cleaned out by those bastards comin' round at night with thousands of yards of bloody nets.'

Neither anglers nor professionals have any respect for fast launches, speed boats, water skiers, or anybody using the waterways for 'pleasure only'. You are permitted, when fishing, to abuse such characters in any language you consider to be appropriate. Shooting them is illegal.

Spear fishermen can occasionally be seen around the Australian coastline. They generally operate off-shore. If you are interested in this sport, take lessons. But first – learn to swim.

Football

Football, as played in Europe, Asia, and Latin America, is also played in Australia, but it is not called football. It is called Soccer – pronounced 'sock 'er'. It should be called 'sock 'im', since a lot of people, players and spectators, do a lot of socking, and the people who do the socking and get socked are nearly always males.

Football as played in America is unknown in Australia. We regard it as being a 'sissy' game, not suitable for men. All those helmets and face guards, and shoulder-pads, and testicle protectors and things. How can you wreck a man's groin or knock his teeth out when you can't get at 'em?

Rugby, as played in England, South Africa and New Zealand – the non-professional 'gentleman's' game – is played in Australia. It is called Union.

The professional, or 'sportsman's' rugby, as played in the North of England, is also played in Australia. It is called League.

But four of Australia's six States play Australian Rules, a game of our own invention, which is called Footy. It draws the biggest crowds, extremely vocal and intensely partisan, and causes the greatest mayhem.

(Mayhem, in case you don't know the word, means 'The maiming of a person by depriving him of the use of any of his members which are necessary for him in defending himself or annoying his adversary' – Webster.)

If you are in Australia for one of our short winters – we are 'the land of sunshine', except when it's raining or snowing – you may wish to attend, or may be invited to attend, one of these four games. (You will not be invited to play.) You should know, therefore, the 'conventional decorum' expected of the spectator.

Sock 'er (or 'im): This game is played with the feet, the hands, the elbows, the knees, the hips, and – the spherical ball is very light – the head. On taking up your position, wait five minutes before voicing any comment. These five minutes will provide you with free health insurance, since you will know, at the expiration of that time, the sentiments of those in your immediate vicinity. Join them in their praise or abuse, and thus avoid injury to your person.

If you feel you *must* disagree with your neighbours vocally, just shout 'kill him' without specifying whom. It will be assumed that you are on the 'right' side.

Also, for this game, you will find some knowledge of abusive phrases in Italian, Greek or Yugoslav very useful.

Union (Old English 'Rugby', or 'Rugger'): Practise etiquette. Never abuse any of the players on either side, and in particular never advocate the execution of the referee. In general, maintain a dignified silence, punctuated occasionally by polite applause with the hands.

For an exceptionally brilliant piece of action, you may say softly, 'Oh, well played, sir.' And for a particularly poor display, shake your head gently, and murmur, 'Dear oh dear oh dear.'

Clap both teams – and the referee – at the conclusion of the game.

League: Each team's objective in this game is to destroy the opposition. The referee's duty is to try to prevent such destruction. Your duty, as a spectator, is to encourage it, and therefore you must frequently express disapproval of the referee. Shout, 'Go home, ya mug', or 'You couldn't referee seven-asiders.'

('Seven-asiders' are games of League played by very small boys, with only seven in each team.)

You may use any phrase that comes to your mind when abusing referees, and your fellow spectators will not object. But they may object if you abuse players for whom they are barracking. As for Soccer, barrack with the majority around you, and avoid getting a beer can, full or empty, on the back of your head.

(Americans should note that word 'barrack'. It is not good etiket to use the word 'root', since its meaning in Australia differs radically from its meaning in America.)

At the end of the game, if the team for which you have been barracking has been defeated, and limps off the field wounded, blood-stained and dejected, always blame the referee.

Footy: Followers of League and Union call this game 'aerial pingpong', or 'ballet dancing'. Do not, under any circumstances, mention these pseudonyms while watching Footy. You may, however, if you are not familiar with the game, announce your ignorance of its rules and objectives.

Two dozen Footy fans will enlighten you. They will then disagree with each other and start fighting. Do not join in. Duck under a seat until the battle is over. If no seat, crawl between legs to another part of the enclosure.

Visitors who intervene in faction fights at Footy will only unite the factions and collect many beer cans.

(*Note*: Beer cans are always used as missiles, never as clubs. And it is not good etiket to throw half-empty cans, since spilt beer could damage the target's clothing, and give offence.)

You will notice that in this game there is no referee. The gentleman with the whistle is called an umpire. His job is to prevent players from committing mayhem on each other with boots, elbows, knees, hips, heads, fists or teeth. He is never very successful, and seldom popular. You may abuse him.

There is a story of an evangelist addressing a Footy crowd during half-time, trying to 'drum up trade' for a Billy Graham crusade. He emphasized that all denominations would be welcome. 'After all,' he said, 'we are all christians, aren't we?' And a voice from the crowd bellowed, 'What about the bloody umpire?'

Footy attracts more spectators than any other sport in Australia. You must never, in Victoria, Tasmania, South Australia or Western Australia – or in parts of the Riverina – decry the game in any way. Always praise it. Footy fans are fanatics, and destructive criticism is suicidal.

Funerals

The late Norman Lindsay, in nearly a hundred years of living, made many hundreds of friends, most of whom died before he did. He attended only two funerals and then swore never to attend another one. He couldn't stand the 'bulldust', the solemn faces, the dark suits and black ties, and the stilted and ritualistic 'expressions of sympathy' required by etiquette.

Funerals are famous for etiquette, which *must* be observed by all attending. The after funeral custom of going back to the home of the deceased for a few grogs is not too bad, but since singing, laughing and 'telling a few yarns' are tabu, the grogs are wasted.

There is no Aussie etiket for funerals. There should be.

'See they're buryin' old Dave this afternoon.'

'Yeah. He died last week. Must be pretty high by now.'

'You goin' to see him off?'

'Yeah. He was me mate. I was with him when the scaffolding fell on him. Why don't you come too? There'll be a bit of a mob there.'

'Aw, I'd have to go home an' change outa these workin' togs.'

'Why? Dave was wearin' workin' togs when the scaffolding fell on him. He'd reckon you were a bit of a ponce if you got dressed up for him.'

'Well – I might come with you. I could do with an afternoon off.'

'Good on ya. It's at his place. His missus's got plenty grog an' tucker, but you c'n bring a couple o' bottles if you like.'

'Goodo. What time?'

'Three o'clock. Get there a bit before to see him off.'

At about three o'clock the official disposer of bodies arrives with transport, and Dave is loaded on.

'So long, mate.'

'Yeah, so long. See you up there.'

'Down there, you mean.'

'Give my regards to St Peter.'

'Give mine to Old Nick.'

The driver takes off for the cemetery – where a hole and a padre are waiting.

'He wasn't a bad poor bastard, the old Dave.'

'No, he was all right. Remember that time you dropped a brick on his foot?'

'Yeah. He was gunna crown me with the larry, but he couldn't catch me hoppin' on one leg.'

'Great bit o' language he let fly with, but.'

'Yeah. He was good on language. Well, let's see how long it takes us to knock that keg off.'

And then the next day, hungover because of Dave's funeral, everybody 'takes a sickie'.

Ah well. While funeral etiquette prevails the best thing to do is to follow Norman Lindsay's custom – don't go.

Golf

Mark Twain once said that golf is the silliest way of going for a walk that was ever invented, or words to that effect.

Maybe for those who live in the bush, that is true. But for city dwellers, golf is better than just walking around suburban streets being barked at by dogs.

The best time to play golf is at daybreak on weekdays, because most people play it at week-ends, and then the course gets cluttered up with women, and others with long handicaps, and it takes you half a day to play eighteen holes.

When following a foursome playing off twenty-plus handicaps, who scatter all over the fairways, and lose balls in the rough, and won't call you through, and when they finally hole out stand around on the green marking their cards and holding post-mortems – which seems to be Aussie etiket for such players – you and your opponent will be tempted to use Aussie words, profane, scatological and expressed in a soft voice with deep feeling. Such temptation should be resisted.

You may, of course, belt a low ball straight at them, shouting, just before it crowns one of them, 'Fore'. Then you march through them, ignoring their indignant or dirty looks. But this practice is frowned upon by committees, and is anyway something like overtaking a smoke-belching semi-trailer on a two-lane winding highway – there's always another one further up the hill.

Play early in the morning on weekdays, thus giving yourself room on the course, and resting your ulcer.

Some golfers say you should play when hungover, because hangovers make you keep your head down. But they spoil your enjoyment of the clean morning air, the dew on the grass, the bird song, that first hole, and that first cigarette. And unless you are a professional, the 'aim of the game' is enjoyment.

Golf is a game for gentlemen and ladies, and the rules of golf conform to the rules of etiquette.

There are, however, a few golfers whose on-course habits are shockingly depraved and difficult to detect; who like to make bets with you; whose smiling faces conceal devilish and devious intent, and about whom visiting players should be warned.

They are few in number, and not generally club members, but below is the advice given to the author by one of them who was a bit tiddley at the time.

('Tiddley' – a condition achieved by knocking back a few at the 19th hole.)

This fellow said:

On the Tee: Always stand on the windward side of your opponent when he is addressing his ball and let cigarette smoke blow across his eyes. Should the wind be from the front or from the rear, or should there be no wind at all, become suddenly inflicted with smokers' cough just as he starts his downswing – but don't forget to apologize.

Watch the flight of his ball carefully and note just where it finishes up in the rough.

On the Fairway: Tell your opponent, as you leave the tee, that you know exactly where his ball is and that you can go straight to it. But make sure you get there first so you can tread on it. Then, after scouting around a little, you can rediscover it, and call out, 'Here it is. Bad luck, mate. It's not a good lie.'

Stay with him until he gets it out onto the fairway, again expressing your sympathy.

Remark, as you walk out of the rough, that he doesn't appear to be swinging as well as usual, and that you think the trouble is with his backswing, which in your opinion seems to be a bit short.

Before his approach shot, remind him to be careful of the bunkers, which you say are deadly.

In the Bunker: When your opponent finds himself in a bunker, tell him the story of the time when *you* were in a bunker and were penalized for grounding your club. This will cause him to address the ball with his club-head too high, and there will be a good chance that he will duff his explosion.

On the Green: Be sure to walk across between your opponent's ball and the pin, planting your heel down firmly into the turf. The depression thus formed will not be noticeable, but it will be enough to deflect his putt from the line.

You now 'have the honour', and your opponent's mood is such that he will begin to force his game.

On the Second Tee: This will be a par 4 hole, calling for a drive and an approach. Use a 3-iron. You will still be able to get on in two and be putting for your birdie. But your opponent will now take a wood and set out to 'show you'. Your chances that he'll slice or hook will be good.

'Now you've got him,' this fellow said. 'He'll be rattled. He'll be forcing all the way around.'

'And what if you're playing with your boss?'

'Gees mate, forget it. You've got to let him win. If he looks like losing, make sure you three-putt a few greens.'

Hospital Visiting

People who have to submit to being 'in-patients' in hospitals are very unfortunate. Even the best of hospitals are lousy places to be in, because of the often painful and always undignified things doctors, surgeons and nurses do to you.

Doctors and surgeons and nurses practise either etiket or etiquette in their private lives, but in hospitals they practise their professions. And the patient is always on the receiving end of their unspeakable practices, and asks every day, 'When can I go home?'

It is not easy to get into hospitals, but it is much harder to get out.

Patients – with one exception – are always very unhappy. The exception applies to married female patients in maternity hospitals or wards, who have had babies. They are generally happy enough, because they are very proud of themselves.

It is a kind, charitable and christian act to visit unhappy patients – but not females who have just had babies. You could easily give the impression that you are the father. Only husbands should visit females who have had babies.

Here then is acceptable hospital-visiting etiket for unhappy patients, male and female:

Male: The unhappy male patient you visit will be your friend, and the purpose of your visit will be to cheer him up.

Normally, if he were miserable at home, you would take him half-a-dozen of the best with which to help him drown his sorrows. But hospitals do not always approve of this cheer-up method. They have rules and regulations, particularly when the patient is on a diet, as he nearly always is. And it is no good trying to smuggle a bottle in to him since there will be no place to hide it, except in the locker alongside his bed. And these lockers are opened frequently by nurses looking for clean pyjamas, and soap, and tooth brushes, and things.

So you go empty-handed. And you see a sign that reads 'No more than two visitors for any one patient. Please do not smoke. Please do not sit on the beds.' Take no notice of this. Sit on the side of his bed, light up a smoke, offer him one, and talk to him.

(The ashtray problem can be solved by using the plastic soap container which you will find in his locker. Empty it out the window before you go.)

After you have settled down comfortably, you smile at him and say, 'Gawd, mate, you're lookin' crook.'

'I am crook,' he'll say. 'If I wasn't crook I wouldn't be here, would I?'

'Makes sense. Hear about old Joe?'

'Joe who?'

'Old Joe from across the road.'

'Him? What about him?'

'He's been crook for weeks.'

'I know that. So what?'

'He died yesterday. Funeral's tomorrow. If it's as stinkin' hot tomorrow as it is today, I'm not goin'. Listen, how would you like a nice big frothy glass of icy-cold ale?'

'Shut up.'

'All right, if that's the way you feel about it. I'm gunna

have a couple as soon as I leave here. What's the tucker like here?'

'Lousy. They've got me on a diet. Just slop. Nothing solid.'

'Gees, you should have been with us Sundy arvo. We had a barbecue. Best T-bone steaks I've ever had. Jacket spuds, salad, Carlton Draught, brown bread'n butter, Red Ned –'

'Shut up.'

'Don't you want to hear about it?'

'No.'

'All right. Hear about Billy Thompson?'

'No.'

'He's in hospital, too. Rolled his car over Saturday night. Not expected to live. Busted all his innards.'

'Shut up.'

'All right. Anything I can do for you, mate?'

'Yes. Just leave me alone and let me go to sleep.'

'Fair enough. You want to get all the sleep you can. Gees, you're lookin' crook.'

And when he shuts his eyes, you empty the soap container out the window, and go to the local, and have a few of the best, and tell the regulars about him. Tell them how crook he is. Tell them they ought to go and cheer him up.

Females: These can be divided into two categories – wives and others.

a. Wives. (With Babies)

If your wife is in a maternity ward, having produced a son and heir, etiket requires that you should visit her. You've 'put up with her' for nine months, through the morning sickness period, through the swollen belly period, through the food fads and fancies period, and through the last month when she was full of complaints, irritable, cranky and nearly impossible to live with. Now she should be flat-bellied again, and beautiful again, and again the girl you loved and married.

This first visit to see her and the baby is a special occasion.

You should wear you suit'n tie. You should carry a large box of chocolates, and a big bunch of flowers. And hope that none of your mates see you.

You will find her lying down with her head and shoulders on three or four pillows, and make-up on her face, and her best and frilliest nightie on, and no bulge under the blanket, and she will indeed look like the girl you loved and married.

She will smile sweetly at you, thank you for the chocolates and flowers, and tell you you shouldn't have spent all that money, and how smart you look, and ask you have you seen the baby.

You say no. And you see the baby. And she says proudly, 'Isn't he beautiful?'

You say, truthfully, 'Strewth. What's wrong with him? His face is all red and screwed up. He looks like a bloody skinned rabbit. Am I the father of that?'

And when you get home, and clean the chocolate and flower petals off your best suit, and cook yourself some bacon and eggs – you don't know how to cook anything else – you say to yourself, 'Bloody women. I'll never understand 'em.'

b. Wives. (Without Babies)

When your wife has had an operation, to fix something that has gone wrong with that complicated internal combustion engine that God gives to all females as a birthday present, she will expect you to visit her *every day*. She will give you nightdresses and bed-jackets and things for you to take home and wash, and a list of things that she wants you to bring her the next day. And she will expect you to remain during the whole of the visiting hour while she tells you all about the doctors and nurses and the other patients.

Etiket requires you to say 'Yes', and 'No' and 'Is that so?' at appropriate intervals, and *not* to keep looking at your watch.

When the bell rings to release you, you feel as though

you have been there for about four hours instead of one. But it is not good etiket to let her know that you would rather be somewhere else.

There is a way to cut the hour down to about ten minutes, and at the same time keep her on side, and even receive her thanks – always forget at least one item on her shopping list. It may be the two oranges, or the three bananas, or the apple, or the fruit knife, or the bottle of lemonade. It doesn't really matter, just forget one item.

She will ask for that forgotten item in the first five minutes. Apologize profusely, saying how busy you have been, and how worried about her, and tell her there is plenty of time – you will go and get it now.

Insist. Go and get it and then head for the nearest pub. Make sure you have some Ombo, or Oraltone, or Peppermint Lifesavers, and keep an eye on your watch. Arrive back in the ward five minutes before the bell, panting from your exertions. Explain that the hospital kiosk didn't have it and that you had to walk and/or run all the way to the shopping centre and try half-a-dozen places before you got it.

She will say, 'Oh, poor you; you shouldn't have bothered', or something similar. But she will be proud of you, because the other ladies in the ward will be impressed by your devotion.

This technique can be varied. You will think of other similarly harmless deceptions, remembering always that you *must* appear to be doing whatever you do only for her.

Others: Other females, such as girl friends, aunts, mothers etc, need only be visited once a week.

Arrive about ten minutes before the bell, apologizing for the traffic jam, the flat tyre, the accident that delayed you because you were required as a witness, your inability to find a parking space within two miles of the hospital, or any other reason that you can think of.

Carry flowers and present them with every sincere expression of sympathy and affection and hopes for a speedy recovery.

The patient will be touched and gratified by your efforts, and by your gift of flowers, and in no time at all you will be out of there, leaving a very favourable impression behind you.

Conclusion: Hospital staffs hate visiting hours, because visiting hours disrupt the practice of their professions. It is therefore good etiket to make your visit as short as possible – and excellent etiket if you can, at the same time, 'cheer up' the patient.

Introductions

Englishmen and Americans are very strong on etiquette when being introduced to you. They have a reputation for politeness, good manners and social grace.

They work to a conventional formula – a system. And it should be stated, here and now, for their information, that their customs are known and understood in Australia. And also, strange as it may seem, often practised by Australians.

We are not famous for politeness, good manners and social grace, but we are capable of these things.

For example, when being introduced to an Englishman, and he hits us with a question – 'How do you do?' – we don't reply with another one, 'How do I do what, mate?' That would wreck his system.

(Englishmen have some weird conventions or systems. When they don't know you, have not been introduced to you, but want to ask you something, they say, 'I say.' And then they shut up and say nothing. If you answer, 'Yes, mate, what do you say?' they become nonplussed and confused.)

Americans generally repeat your name when you are introduced to them. But they also ask a question. They say, 'How do you do Mr McGillicuddy?' This is a rude and

47

anatomical enquiry, and if we answered it we would demonstrate that we are ignorant of their formula. Which we are not. We know that they like to remember people's names, so they make sure they hear them twice – once on being introduced and once when they ask their biological question.

There exists, however, a native-Australian etiket for introductions, which is honest, genuine, sincere, forthright and informal, and which you Poms and Yanks should know about. A few lines of dialogue will clue you up:

'G'day Smithy. Like you to meet a new mate o' mine. He's a Pom.'

'Well, that probably wasn't his fault. Howyergoin' mate, orright?'

The Pom is silent.

'Don't talk much, does he? What'd you say yer name was?'
'Charles Tebbutt.'

'Charles? You hear that, Mick? Bloody Charles. Orright, we got it. What'd you like a drop of, Chick?'

A few more lines of dialogue:

'Hey Cec, come over 'ere and meet a mate o' mine, name of Ed Miller. Ed – this is Cec.'

'Pleased to meet you.'

'How do you do, Cec?'

'Ed's from America.'

'Yeah? What's a bloody Septic Tank doin' out here? Never mind – what're you drinkin', Dusty?'

And again:

'Joey, meet Jean. Jean – this is Joey.'

She extends her hand. She says, 'How do you do?'

'Doin' all right, love, long as I got your hand to hang onto. Gees, mate, where did you dig her up?'

'Met her at a party last week.'

'Wish I'd been there. I'da got in first.'

'Well, let her hand go, will you? It's mine.'

Got the picture? Honest, genuine, sincere, forthright and informal.

Loving Thy Neighbour

In America the place where you live is known as the 'neighbourhood'. In Australia it is just known as the place where you live.

Neighbourhood is a cumbersome word, and although we know what it means, we don't normally use it. But we do use the word 'neighbour'. And by custom and usage, when we refer to our neighbour we mean the fellow who lives alongside of us, one side or the other.

(It is not true that the word has evolved from the verb to neigh, as in horse, although some neighbours do make similar noises.)

It is commanded, on highest authority, that 'Thou shalt love thy neighbour'. But it must be remembered that the 'love' referred to is an English translation of an ancient pre-English word used by Moses and his tribes, and is for application to men only.

Neighbour is a masculine noun. 'Thou shalt not covet thy neighbour's wife' is another commandment brought down by Moses from the mountain. Therefore we are not permitted to love the missus of the bloke next door. And in the broader definition of the word neighbour, where it means 'all mankind' – black, white, brown, yellow and brindled – there is no mention of womankind.

Aussie etiket, which controls our relationships with our neighbours, continues this discrimination. And wisely so. The man who starts 'goin'' for' his neighbour's woman can buy himself a whole truckful of real trouble, physical and financial.

Our 'conventional decorum', therefore, in our daily, weekly, or monthly confrontations with neighbouring females, is influenced by the Commandments of Moses, the Epistles of St Paul, and the Philosophy of Plato. And English-speaking migrants who settle in Australian communities must, if they wish to remain vertical and solvent, remember this. Your neighbour is a man. And you must, at all times, extend to him your charitable and platonic 'love'.

(If you are a female, your 'neighbour' will be a woman. Give your love to her only.)

'Do unto others as you would have them do unto you' is the drill. It is not always easy. A neighbour can do some shocking things to you. As under:

a. His car has been playing up. He needs it to go to work in the morning. He thinks the trouble is in the carburettor.

He sets his alarm for four o'clock in the morning. At four-o-five he gets his car out of the garage – carbon monoxide can kill him – parks it alongside your bedroom window and starts revving it up, making adjustments to his carby as he revs.

You will be permitted to stick your head out of your window and yell, 'What the bloody hell do you think you're bloody doin' you inconsiderate bastard?'

You have to yell because the revving is making a lot of noise. And although you may not be accustomed to using the words 'bloody' and 'bastard' so early in the morning, you remember that bloody is the 'great Australian adjective', and that bastard is a 'term of endearment'. You are interested in what he is doing and you want to find out about it. And that is a very 'loving' thing to do.

b. His lawn needs mowing. The only time he has for this job is at the week-end. And his neighbour – you – who, as he knows, practises loving him, is sure to offer to help him by raking up the grass, or 'trimming the edges', or something. He wants to spare you this labour. He knows that you always have a roast dinner on Sundays, about one o'clock, and after it you like to go to sleep for a couple of hours. Now you can't rake up grass or trim edges or something while you're asleep, can you? So that, he reckons, is the best time for him to mow his lawn.

Whether he uses a buzz-bomb petrol-driven mower, or a high-whining electric one, is unimportant. The important thing is that he shows his love for his neighbour by doing the job while you're asleep.

c. He comes home very late from his club – say about two o'clock in the morning. His original intention, as he told his wife, was to be home about six-thirty, or at least no later than seven. She had his evening meal ready for him at that time. But how was he to know that he would get tangled up with old mates whom he hadn't seen for years?

His dinner, which his wife had kept hot for him until nine o'clock, is now charcoal. And she is really burning.

Now etiket says that when a wife is burning, and telling you many things about yourself that you didn't know before, you should refrain from comment. You should remove yourself from 'the way of temptation'. But it is too late to go back to the club.

So he takes two cold bottles – it is better to give than to receive – and visits you.

When you respond to the ringing, banging and kicking at your door, he tells you that you are looking very bleary-eyed and unhappy, obviously in need of some cold refreshment and conversation.

You deny this and tell him that you think he should go to bed. Your consideration for his welfare touches his heart and he loves you more than ever. He wants to do something for you.

So he takes you into your own kitchen, and while you are reluctantly sharing the bottles with him, he proceeds to cook you some supper. You say you don't want it. You say, 'At two-thirty in the morning? Eat it your bloody self.'

He does so because he doesn't want you to come into your kitchen at seven o'clock and find a plateful of cold chops and eggs there.

And then, because he loves you, and doesn't want to embarrass you, he lets you do something for him. He lies down in your living-room and asks you for a couple of blankets.

(Note: During a kind and thoughtful visit of this nature you will notice that your wife does not appear. She is keeping out of 'the way of temptation' by not coming out of the bedroom to talk to you. She knows that you and your neighbour wish to be alone, sharing your love for each other. She will talk to *his* wife in the morning.)

d. You have often mentioned to your neighbour that one of these days you would like to pull out your old sash-type bedroom window, enlarge the aperture, and put in slidingglass. He thinks about this, and early one morning when he wakes up and can't get back to sleep again he decides that it would be a very neighbourly and loving thing to do to help you.

It is summertime and daylight about four o'clock. He gets up, and using a steel 'point' and a four-pound hammer, starts knocking out bricks.

You wake up and object loudly, using many 'bloodies' and

'bastards', and tell him, for the love of Mike – your other neighbour – to knock it off and go back to bed. He says he's been in bed. He says you should go back to bed and he'll carry on.

He does so. And will continue to do so until, or unless, you forcibly remove him.

If there should be a big storm that afternoon, with much wind and driving rain, and your wall-to-wall carpet and your bed should get very wet, he will offer to let you and your wife sleep on the floor of his living-room.

e. He keeps a barking dog. A Pomeranian or a Dachshund. He is an animal lover; he thinks that the sound of a small dog barking through the night will be as music in your ears and cause you to smile with happiness and contentment.

When you tell him in the morning that his bloody dog kept you awake all night, and say, 'Can't you shut the damn thing up?' he knows that you are only trying to avoid a display of sentimental affection for it.

f. He has a big heap of prunings and grass clippings, partly dried out, in his backyard. He will set fire to the heap, sending smoke and ashes streaming on the wind into your place, when your wife is hanging out her washing.

To love such a neighbour, to be kind and considerate and helpful towards him, is difficult. But to throw dead cats on his lawn, or empty your garbage tin on it, is not good etiket. Do him a favour. Mow it for him – at three-thirty some Sunday morning.

Motoring

Australians are required by law to drive as near as possible to the left-hand side of the road, and to give way at all times to any vehicle approaching from the right. This latter requirement causes many accidents, since to be able to observe at all times any vehicle approaching from your right you would need a third eye in your right earhole.

And there is no driver insurance that will provide you with the funds to pay the doctors for trying to cure the fibrositis in your neck.

Until this law is modified, or repealed, it is good etiket to swear about it, privately and publicly, on any occasion or in any company – preferably while conversing with the Prime Minister, State Premiers, Ministers for Transport, Officials of Automobile Clubs and Associations, Commissioners of Police, and Members of the Gravediggers and Undertakers' Assistants' Union.

A good opening gambit when in confrontation with any of the above is to poke him in the chest with a stiff forefinger and say, 'Now listen, sport, what's wrong with you bastards?'

Englishmen have no trouble with the Aussie rules of motoring. But Americans do. Americans down on R and R from South-East Asia, are, at the time of writing, forbidden to drive in Australia. They are only with us for five days and that is not considered long enough for them to learn and become accustomed to our peculiar driving habits.

'There are times up there when you get a little scared,' one said to the author's wife. 'But I ain't never been so scared as I was today.'

'Why? What happened?'

'That old guy drives like a bat out o' hell on the wrong side the goddam road. He wants to commit suicide is okay by me. But I wanted out, an' he jest wouldn't stop.'

Worse things could happen to him. He could go back and finish his stint in the Army and then emigrate to Australia, take a few lessons and bone up on the Rules of the Road, and then get himself a driver's licence. And he would find on our roads suicidal maniacs who would make his elderly chauffeur look like the black-suited driver of a hearse.

Here, young Mr America, are some of the things they will do to you:

At sixty miles per hour on a highway they will sit three feet from your rear bumper 'getting a tow'.

With four surf boards on top, and a P-plate on the stern, they will overtake you at seventy knots, distributing empty coke bottles, beer cans, apple cores and real live cigarette butts as they go.

They will grip the steering wheel with clenched fists and drive at twenty miles per hour as near as possible to the *right* – the centre line. (In these cases they will be wearing hats.)

They will make a right-hand turn from a left-hand lane – or vice versa – cutting across your bows just as you start moving.

They will hit the brakes and swerve all over the road because a bee has just flown in their window.

They will try to 'hedge hop' their way past a long line of cars following two semi-trailers and a truck full of blue metal, cutting in and making you brake to avoid damage to your starboard side for'ard fender.

They will pull out to overtake you and then duck in again, making you accelerate to avoid damage to your starboard side rear tail light.

They will sit in front of you, a few feet behind a big fuel tanker, and send you cross-eyed as they weave in and out trying to see whether or not they can overtake. (While they're doing this, you drop back to give them room to drop back so they can see, and a long-hair with a dolly bird in his pocket burns into the space.)

And always, for the whole of your journey, because you are driving safely, you will be abused with sentences like 'Bloody mug, why don't you buy a bike?' or 'Where did you get your bloody licence, Woolworth's?'

It is the opinion of every Australian driver that all others are idiots. There is only one good one. Himself.

In fact ninety per cent of Aussie drivers are good. They obey restrictive speed signs. They give way to the right and watch for galahs on their left. They drive one car's length behind the vehicle in front for every ten miles per hour of speed. And if some gherkin cuts in they just drop back saying quietly, 'My goodness.' They signal their intentions to overtake, stop or turn. They leave themselves room to manoeuvre in case an accident happens further up the line. They let any ratbag overtake them at any speed if he wants to.

But what do they do on a two-lane road, approaching a right-hand bend, when some candidate for the next world comes roaring round straight at them, overtaking a truck? Here they use Aussie etiket. They shout loudly, 'You stupid prawn-headed mullet-gutted idiot bastard,' at the same time changing down a cog or two and heading for the bush.

It is possible to do the right thing at all times and still

be killed. There is, however, one way to avoid death and improve your state of health – walk. Walk well away from any road frequented by automobiles. And by the time you have walked, say, from Sydney to Perth, or from Melbourne to Darwin, you will be the fittest Yank in the South Pacific. And you won't need a walker's licence.

Picnicking

'Goin' on a picnic', or 'havin' a picnic lunch' is an old Australian custom, practised mainly in the summer-time when there are plenty of little bush flies about.

Picnics are greatly loved by women and kids and detested by all Australian male adults.

The Man of the House is expected to drive the car, 'find a good spot', light the fire, make the brew – 'billy tea' – organize kids' games and/or supervise swimming, accept personal responsibility for all sunburn, cuts, abrasions and insect bites, stop all fights, watch his language, display forbearance and patience when told, 'No, you're not having another beer – you're driving,' put the fire out, clean up all the rubbish, and drive home with a car full of tired and irritable kids and nagging females, on a highway infested with 'bloody Sunday drivers', all of whom should, in his opinion, be locked up and certified insane.

Another man in the picnic party will provide him with some spiritual comfort and moral support, and if you are invited it will be for this reason. Consequently, in any discussion you must never support women and/or kids at any time, even should you think they are right.

Conversely, you must never support your host vocally since by doing so you will make enemies of the women and kids – they can be very dangerous enemies indeed.

Support your host silently and help him in his many tasks, and thereby earn his friendship and esteem. You may speak in praise of his billy tea, strong and black and smoky and full of tannin and guaranteed to 'take the lining off a cast-iron gut', by saying, as you sip it cautiously, 'Good brew, this.'

Praise the food – the cold corned beef, the cold hogget, the melting butter, the stale bread, the pickled onions etc – so tastefully set out by the women, as you brush away the flies and ants and multitude of other insects which will be unknown to you.

Offer to help with the tidying up. And when you get back to your host's home, help him to drink the beer he wasn't permitted to drink previously, and make a resolution, which you may embody in a toast which the women won't understand because of the foreign language, but which *he* will understand in any language – 'Barbecue da, piknik niet.'

Pie Eating

Hot meat pies with tomato sauce are found only in Australia, and they are found all over the continent.

They are magnificent food and 'marry' well with beer. It is permitted to eat one or two off a plate, using a knife and fork, and with a cup of tea on the side. But without tuition you will have difficulty in consuming one while standing up with a glass of beer in your hand.

Pies are juicy, and tomato sauce is runny, and neither juice – gravy – nor sauce will be welcome in your neighbour's beer, and either or both will look unpleasant on your chin or your shirt.

Take the pie, therefore, in your right hand, with a couple of thicknesses of paper under it, because it will be very hot. (Toilet paper will do, if no other is available.)

Hold it then at an angle of about ten degrees and carefully bite out a piece of the crisp upper edge, exposing the interior meat and gravy, or juice. Apply this preliminary opening to your lips, and suck. As the gravy content diminishes you may bite off more of the edge and progress gradually towards the centre.

Tomato sauce is licked off as you go, to prevent it from running down that ten-degree slope into your hand.

You will earn considerable respect, if not applause, when you can eat a whole pie without dropping sauce or gravy anywhere. Practise in your bathroom.

Having finished the pie, etiket decrees that you should wipe your lips with the paper, crumple it up, and drop it at your feet amongst the cigarette butts, there to be swept up later by the pub staff.

Note for Americans: Tomato is pronounced 'tomahto' – and tomato sauce is never referred to as 'ketchup'. Ask for 'pie'n tomahto sauce'.

In some pubs you can get 'pie'n peas', or 'pie'n pertater'. These are made by lifting the lid of the pie and inserting a spoonful of peas or mashed spuds before heating. Suck as for 'pie'n tomato sauce'.

'Pies'n vegs', if offered, will be served on a plate, with a knife and fork.

South Australians, especially during their short winters, are fond of a thing called a 'floater'. If you want to know what it's like, suck it an' see.

(Note for Englishmen: The Australian meat pie is the greatest contribution ever offered to the stomachs of mankind since the Chinese invented roast pork. It in no way resembles, the Lord be praised, your mince pie or abominable cold pork pie. Taste and texture are entirely different. But, although you may not have experienced the delightful and incomparable gastronomic joy incorporated into the Aussie meat pie, you will probably recognize your country's influence on the development of the South Australian 'floater'. In Liverpool, and other Lancastrian places north-west of London, you will have enjoyed 'lobscouse 'n chips' – a sort of thin stew with chips floating in or on it. A 'floater' is 'scouse'n pie'. How to eat it is your problem.)

Playing the Pokies

Poker machines, or 'one-armed bandits' – perhaps known to you as fruit machines, or slot machines – are, as this is being written, illegal in five of the six Australian States. They are legal only in New South Wales, and only in clubs. Pubs are not permitted to have them. They make big profits, which, even after the New South Wales Government drains a few millions off in taxes, build bigger clubs, with more and more amenities, and accommodating thousands of members. They return to the players only a little over ninety per cent of the capital invested through their slots, so in the long run nobody wins except the management committees and the Government.

Should you wish to learn the etiket of pokie manipulation, stand by, watch and listen.

The dedicated player arms himself with plenty of coins and waits for a vacant machine. He needs plenty of coins, because if he leaves the machine to go back to the bar for some more, somebody else will move in on it.

Having moved in himself on a temporarily vacant one, he begins feeding his coins into it, using the 'firm strong pull', the 'clean and jerk' as in weight-lifting, the 'slowly applied pressure' pull, or a combination of all three. During this operation he will talk to himself, at fifteen-minute intervals, as under:

'You useless bastard of a bloody thing.'

'Shit, that was close.'

'Ha. You bloody little beauty.' (When a few coins rattle into the tin.)

'Come on. Come on. COME ON.'

'Gawd, you wouldn't read about it.'

'Gees, it would happen to me.'

When he puts in his last coin, he says, 'That's the last. Now, you bitch of a thing. Pay off.'

The machine goes clunk clunk clunk – and is then silent.

The player says, 'Man's a bloody idiot,' and goes to borrow his taxi fare home from the barman.

A waiting player moves in, puts his first coin in the slot, pulls the lever nonchalantly, and is rewarded with a deluge of coins. 'JACKPOT,' he yells.

And your player looks as though he is about to cry, but becomes angry instead, and says, 'You flukey tin-arse bastard.'

Playing the pokies can make you, in etiket language, a. 'crooked on' your fellow players, or b. 'crooked on' yourself.

It is good that there are no pokies in pubs. A man does enough dough at the bar without one-armed bandits reefing it off him.

Pubs

The word 'pub' is an abbreviation of the English public-house. And with few exceptions Australian pubs are modelled on English public-houses, because the first unwilling migrants to our country were English – with a few Irish, Scots and Welsh brought out as ballast.

In our cities there are a few foreign-style taverns, bars, club bars, restaurant bars, bistros and plonk shops. But mainly, all over Australia, there are pubs.

Pubs are required by law to provide, in addition to alcoholic beverages, food and accommodation.

Visiting or migrant Englishmen will find our pubs much like their own at home. Visiting or migrant Americans will need some briefing. They will need some instruction in the etiket of pub behaviour.

In your own country, Mr American, you can take a 'tomato', or a 'dog', or even a 'lady' into a bar or tavern, and sit down at a table and demand alcohol and/or food at any time when the door is open, say up to three or four in the morning. You 'can't do that there 'ere.'

There are specified hours for food, and when the 'tucker's off' you won't get any. And most bars close at ten o'clock.

And if you take a lady into a public bar you won't make any friends, and will probably be refused service.

Legally, women are permitted in any part of a pub except the gents, but an unwritten law excludes them from public bars. This unwritten law does not apply to barmaids, which is what everybody calls them, although officially they are styled 'bar attendants'.

Every pub has its public bar, which is all-male territory – so don't take dolls in. There are saloon bars and lounges where females will be welcome. Some words about dress:

Dress rules are laid down by pub managements, and in saloon and lounge areas vary considerably. Some managements will refuse you service if you are not wearing a jacket and tie. Some insist on shoes. Some couldn't care less.

Generally speaking, city publicans are fussy, and have strict rules; suburban and country publicans are not, and don't.

When in doubt, approach some character who is just leaving or entering, and ask him – using this conventional phrase:

'Excuse me, mate – I've got a sheila with me, an' we want to slurp up a few grogs. Does the bastard who runs this joint expect a bloke to wear a coat an' tie?'

Be guided by the answer, which you may trust. It will be given seriously and with complete honesty. Australians are great leg-pullers, but no single one of us would 'steer you wrong' in answer to any question connected with grog or the etiket attached to its consumption.

(About that word 'sheila'. The words 'bird', 'dolly bird', 'crumpet', 'bit of homework', 'tomato', 'dog', 'dame', 'charlie', 'skirt', 'week-ender', etc, are known and understood in Australia. But sheila is a general word, embracing all ages, from consent to senility.)

All right – supposing you are very hot, tired, dirty and

thirsty; the marks of your 'eight hours work for eight hours pay' are all over you; your face is streaked with sweat and grime; your shorts and shirt are stained with creosote, cement, paint, bitumen and brick dust; your rag hat is drooping limply around your ears; your boots have been hurting you, so you have taken them off and hung them around your neck by the laces; and you need – badly need – half-a-dozen containers of ice-cold amber refreshment, with no more than a half-inch of head.

What to do? Ask somebody leaving or entering about dress? Never. Go into the public bar and feel at home. Somebody – maybe even dirtier than you – will say, 'Gees, mate, you look buggered. I'm in the chair. What'll you have?'

You say, 'Thanks, mate. The same as you.'

And you're amongst friends. *But* – and this is very important – when it comes to your turn, return the 'shout'. Otherwise the word will spread that you are a 'bludger', and there is no worse thing to be. You just say, 'My shout', and pay up.

After a few rounds you'll need the toilet, which is called the gents. And there is a recognized etiket for your behaviour in this place. You do not stand in front of the porcelain pews, or stainless steel trough, and ignore your neighbour. You are expected to acknowledge his presence. Any one of the following three opening sentences will do:

'Gees, this is a relief.'

'A man's just a go-between, isn't he? In one end and out the other.'

'How do you stop these things?'

Such remarks will lead to a minute or two of pleasant, friendly conversation, and then you should return to your 'possie' at the bar.

It is *not* good form to visit the gents and then leave the pub without saying goodbye to your casual drinking companions. Formal goodbyes, such as 'Thank you very much, gentlemen, for the pleasure of your company' are okay in saloon bars and lounges, but will earn you unfavourable comment in public bars. A simple 'Well, that'll do me for now – be seein' ya' is all that is required. Provided it's not your shout.

A newcomer we know once went into a public bar and asked for a dry martini.

The barmaid laughed, and said, 'Now pull the other one.'

He said, 'Huh? Pull the other what?'

'Leg,' she said.

He said, 'I don't get it.'

'That's right,' she said. 'You don't get it.'

This caused him to be silent.

'Well, come on,' she said. 'Make up your mind. What do you want?'

He said, 'A dry martini, please.'

One of the locals said, 'I think he's fair dinkum, Mabs.'

And she said, 'He's fair dinkum bonkers, if you ask me.'

And she went away to serve somebody else.

It is not good etiket to ask for cocktails in public bars. And anyway, you won't get one. Play safe. Stick to beer.

Speech Making

Every Australian, at some time in his life, is called upon to make a speech or propose a toast. If you are a new arrival in our land you will certainly be called upon, and you should know the correct etiket.

You need not necessarily be witty, erudite and informative, although a judicious injection into your speech of any or all of these things will be appreciated. You must never be long-winded like a politician. Keep your speech reasonably short; but above all let it be honest, sincere, genuine and from the heart. Australians are quick to detect phoniness in any shape or form. 'Bulldust' is bad etiket.

Perhaps the easiest way to explain good speech-making etiket would be to give you an example. The following sincere, genuine, and from the heart speech is therefore reprinted, for your earnest study, from Nino Culotta's book *Gone Fishin'*. The occasion was Denis' engagement party, and Joe was called upon to propose the toast. He said:

'Ladies an' gentlemen, ut's my duty to propose the toast of Jeannie an' Denis, the reason bein' that that hunk o' rock on Jeannie's finger means they're engaged. I dunno why. Den's been me mate for a long time. Up to now he's always

managed to keep out o' trouble. He's had hundreds o' sheilas
in 'is time, but none of 'em ever hooked 'im permanent. So
don't count on this one. One time we thought 'e was gunna
marry Nino's sister. Another time we thought 'e was gunna
marry a little German sheila by the name o' Renate. That's
the one 'e should'a married, in my opinion. She was a little
bottler. Why *didn't* yer marry 'er, Den? – Eh? – Can't hear
yer. Well, I reckon ut *is* my business. Looked after yer, didn't
I, in all them foreign countries where yer couldn't speak
the language. If ut hadn't been for me yer'd never've got
home. Be still stuck in a sidin' somewhere in bloody Germany.
Who's swearin'? There's ladies present. Would I be swearin'
with ladies present? Now where was I? – Yeah. About
gettin' married. I reckon y'oughta give ut some thought. Yer
don't want to go doin' anything yer goin' to be sorry for later.
Yer not the marryin' kind, matey. Bein' married c'n get yer
down, yer know. There's a lot o' worries in ut. Look wot
'appened to Nino. Worried 'imself into gettin' crook an' havin'
to knock off work an' go fishin'. If 'e 'adn't been married 'e
wouldn't've got crook, an' 'e wouldn't've gone fishin', an' we
wouldn't've gone with 'im, an' you wouldn't've met Jeannie,
an' yer wouldn't be trapped now. Never thought o' that, did
yer? I *am* proposin' the bloody toast, ain't I? Yer can't
just say yer propose a toast. Yer gotta make a bit of a
speech. That's wot you asked me to do, wasn't ut, Shorty?
So orright, well. So gimme a go. Another thing. Mullet.
That's wot she'll feed you on, yer know. She was reared on
ut. An' there's one thing definite I know about women. Yer
can't change their habits. Look at Edie. Fish 'n chips every
Fridy night. Yer know wot you'll get, don't yer? You'll get
mullet every bloody day. Ut's only fit for bait, matey. You
ever seen this family sit down to a decent feed o' steak an'
eggs? So orright. So you know wot yer in for. Now I gotta
tell Jeannie somethin' about you. He's a builders' labourer,
Jeannie. Been one all 'is life, an' always will be one. You

believe all this talk about 'im wantin' to be an articheck? I don't. An' I've known 'im longer than you.'

The Old Man interrupted. 'Finish hup with the harse hout of 'is pants.'

'Eh? Like hell 'e will. You wouldn't get a better worker anywhere than the old Den. An' wot's more, he's honest. An' if 'is mate's in trouble, he sticks with 'im. Not like some old blokes around 'ere. Who's insinuatin'? I'm insinuatin' nothin'. I'm bloody tellin' yer. He's only got one fault; he likes to bung on an act. An' e's bungin' one on now. All this pommy talk, an' wantin' to be an articheck. He's havin' you on, Jeannie. Don't you fall for ut. If 'e marries you I'll eat a bloody mullet meself. Man couldn't be fairer than that, could 'e? Well, that's all I gotta say. So I'll ask yer to charge yer glasses, be upstandin', an' drink the toast o' Jeannie an' Denis.'

A perfect speech and perfect etiket.

Telephoning

'Heaven,' my friend Dave reckons, 'is when your telephone breaks down and you can't get anybody to come and fix it.' Alexander Graham Bell, he says, should have been drowned at birth.

Australia, like all other so-called civilized nations, suffers from a plague of these electronic nuisances and perpetual disturbers of the peace of its citizens.

The plague is endemic and apparently incurable. It spreads its virus through thousands of tons of copper wire, stretched on millions of ugly poles, from Sydney to Perth, from Hobart to Darwin.

There is a telephone etiquette – international – which some Australians practise. There is an Aussie etiket – national – which most Australians practise.

English gentlemen, and polite Americans, will be familiar with the first. (Except that Americans, having got their number, say, 'Is this Mister Jones?' and Australians say, 'Is that you, Jonesy?' The Aussie question makes sense. If Jones is five hundred miles away he can't be a 'this' – he has to be a 'that'. And 'Jonesy' is friendlier than 'mister'.)

But English gentlemen and polite Americans will need

some introduction to Aussie telephone etiket, which, if encountered without prior knowledge of it, could send them around the bend. Some examples:

Business: You ring a business firm and etiquette says that a warm, sexy, contralto, female voice will say, 'Good morning, Mineral Investments. May I help you?'

(If it should be two o'clock in the afternoon, that will be because she is putting polish on her nails, and is a little absent-minded. Do not remind her that it is afternoon.)

You say, 'My name is Pomeroy – Rodney Pomeroy – and I would like to make an appointment to see Mister Jones, at his convenience.'

She says – in a voice that sends shivers up and down your spine – 'Mister Jones is busy on another line. May I ring you back?'

You give her your number and she rings back within five minutes, and tells you that Mr Jones will be happy to see you at eleven o'clock tomorrow morning.

Etiket is different. You ring. And you hear buzz-buzz, buzz-buzz, buzz-buzz for at least ten minutes.

Then a flat, nasal, soprano voice says, 'Hullo?'

You say, very politely, 'Hullo to you too.'

'Wot?' the voice says.

'I said — hullo to you too.'

'I heard yer. You tryin' to be funny?'

'No – really I'm not. Is that (or this) Mineral Investments?'

'Yeah. 'Course it is. Wotta yer want?'

'I would like to make an appointment to see Mister Jones, at his convenience.'

'Well yer can't. He's busy.'

'Well – could you ask his secretary to make an appointment for me, please?'

'No. She's gone to lunch.'

'Oh. I see. Well – how can I get to make an appointment with him?'

'How would I know? Write him a letter.'

Don't argue. It will get you nowhere. Write him a letter.

Government Departments: Forget etiquette. Aussie etiket applies.

Give yourself an hour first to sort out the confusion in what you think is the appropriate section in the telephone directory. Keep your fingers crossed and dial what you consider to be the appropriate number.

Buzz-buzz, buzz-buzz, buzz-buzz, buzz-buzz. Be patient. It is probably morning – or afternoon – tea-time. Wait fifteen minutes. Then hang up and dial the number again.

If you are lucky you will only have to wait a further ten minutes before you hear a click and a voice. A bored and disinterested voice says, 'Department of Confusion. Hold the line, please.'

You hold it for fifteen minutes. You start swearing. You think, 'To hell with them. I'll write a letter.'

You are about to hang up when the bored and disinterested voice says, 'Department of Confusion.'

'Oh – thank you. I would like to speak to someone in authority, please.'

'Who's calling?'

'R. Pomeroy.'

'A Pommy?'

'My name is R – R for Rodney – Pomeroy.'

'What is the purpose of your enquiry, please?'

(Public servants often say please. They are trained that way. When they tell you to 'fill in the form, please' the 'please' means that if you don't 'fill in the form' you will get 'no-bloody-where'.)

'What is the purpose of your enquiry, please?'

'I prefer to tell that to someone in authority.'

'Oh. Just a minute.'

Click. You wait twenty of those minutes. You hang up. You've got 'no-bloody-where'. Write a letter.

After a couple of months you could even get an answer. If the PMG mob are not on strike.

Incoming Calls: It is astonishing when you think of the number of people who ring you up at inconvenient times, such as when you are watching the TV News or an episode of 'Steptoe and Son', or are half way through your dinner, which gets cold while you talk to the characters.

And even at convenient times, incoming calls can increase your blood pressure and cause you to use words condemned by etiquette. Like this one:

'Five seven eight one three seven O'Grady.'

'Oh – Is that Mister O'Grady?'

You have already said so, but you don't abuse him because his voice is heavily accented, and etiket says we must be kind and forbearing in our relations with foreigners.

So you just answer quietly, 'Yes.'

And he says, 'You are the friend of the lady Iris Harding?'

'The lady who?'

'Iris Harding.' He pronounces it very clearly.

'Never heard of her, mate.'

'She is living in Oatley, near to you, yes?'

'She might be. But I don't know her.'

'She is your friend.' It is not a question. It is a statement.

'Sorry mate. I think you must have the wrong number.'

And you hang up.

Five minutes later the 'phone rings again. Same character. Same conversation.

When it rings the third time, you've had him. You say, 'Listen sport, get lost will you? You've got the wrong number.' And you hang up on him.

Five minutes later the thing rings again. You decide to

ignore it. But it keeps ringing, and it wears you down. You work out a completely devastating four-word sentence to hit him with, and pick up the receiver. Before you can say the first of the four words, a native-born Australian female voice says, 'Hullo, Mister O'Grady.'

You are charmed. And disarmed. You don't know the voice, but that doesn't mean you don't know its owner. You play it safe. You say 'Hullo, love.'

And she says, 'This is St George Hospital. Do you know a barmaid named Sunny?'

'Sunshine? Yes. How's she getting on?'

'She's ready to go home. Could you come and get her?'

You've known Sunshine – or Sunny – or Sunny Jim, who pours it out for you in the local pub, for nearly twenty years. But how the hell are you supposed to know her name is Harding? You didn't even know it was Iris.

Outgoing Calls: Don't make any. Write letters. Join the revolution. Put bumper bar and rear-window stickers on your car – 'Ban Telephones. Write Letters.' And then the abominable things could, in a few years, die of starvation.

Transport

People always seem to be wanting to go from one place to some other place, and nobody wants to walk. A few, like postmen, ride bikes. A few, like stockmen in Queensland, the Northern Territory, and the Kimberleys, ride horses. But the rest of us, millions of us, want engines.

We want motor-cycles, or scooters, or cars, or taxis, or trains, or trucks, or semi-trailers, or buses, or ferries, or aeroplanes – or we even, as in Melbourne, want trams. And all of these things are noisy, and with the exception of trams, all pollute our beautiful eucalyptus-scented atmosphere.

(Trams balance their lack of stinking exhausts by being twice as noisy as anything else that runs on land or water. You will notice, if you try to describe the joys and delights of Sydney, that Melbourne people are all deaf.)

Should you be neither a postman nor a stockman, and are travelling by scooter, motor-cycle, car, truck, or semi-trailer, behave as advised in the section headed 'Motoring'. For the etiket, or etiquette, in other forms of transport, see under:

Taxis: These are recognizable by their multi-colours, and by signs on top that light up and read 'Taxi'. It is sometimes possible to hail one as it is cruising, and sometimes its driver may pull in to you and stop. In which case get in before he changes his mind.

But the best way of getting a taxi is to walk to a taxi rank. There you approach the first car on the rank. Do this quietly, because the driver will be reading a newspaper, or paperback, or gazing into space thinking about things, and it is not good etiket to frighten him. Cough gently until you get his attention. You will know you have his attention when he looks at you. Then get in and sit down.

He will then say, 'Where to?'

You tell him, and he will say, 'Gawd, it would happen to me.' Or he might mutter to himself, 'Gees, I don't go that far on me bloody holidays.'

At the end of the journey, add ten per cent to the fare and say, 'Thanks, driver.' He will then cheer up a little, and his 'Thanks, mate' will be friendly. If he has a European accent he may even say 'Thank you, sir.'

You could, of course, pay him the exact fare as shown on the meter, offering a note of large denomination and waiting for the change. He won't say anything then, but your character, and the characters of your ancestors, will be vividly summed up in adequate language when he is fraternizing with other drivers.

Buses: Some buses are run by private enterprise. The private enterprises that run these buses will not admit to making a profit, and are always asking for things called subsidies. But most buses are run by Governments.

Governments admit to losing money on buses, and these losses have to be made up by taxpayers. Government buses are big machines and very noisy. They have fundamental orifices under their starboard quarters, from which they blurt horrible black gases that make people cough and sneeze and use bad language.

But you must not use bad language when travelling *in*

buses. Bus conductresses and conductors are ladies and gentlemen, whose delicate ears are not accustomed to hearing profane words. Should you inadvertently use a few, they will stop the bus, and ask you politely to get out. Should you refuse to get out they will not permit the bus to start again.

This pleases the driver who then has a little sleep. But it does not please other passengers who want to go somewhere else, and you will be forced to leave the bus because you are outnumbered.

You may then use bad language without penalty – provided there are no policemen about.

When riding in buses it is good etiket to say nothing and read a newspaper. Large newspapers are best. They may annoy your neighbour by flapping across his face when you are turning the pages, but they are good to hide behind when elderly or pregnant ladies come aboard looking for seats.

It is not good etiket to give your seat to a lady, since most ladies say they believe in 'Women's Lib', and it is your duty to instruct them in its meaning. Large newspapers help you to provide this instruction in a dignified and silent manner.

When travelling in cities from up-town to down-town, or vice versa, it is not a good idea to travel in buses. Walking is quicker.

Aircraft: This word means the same as aeroplane, but is considered more suitable in English-speaking countries, since aeroplane is French.

Nevertheless, when in an aircraft you will be required to practise French etiquette. Captains and first-officers are gentlemen who practise etiquette at all times – when the PA is switched on.

And hostesses – never call them stewardesses as in the USA – are ladies, who call you 'Sir', or 'Madam', provided they can tell the difference. They never say, 'Hey you' or 'Want a grog, sport?' or offer coffee and biscuits with the words, 'Here, get that into you.' They use etiket only between themselves when in the galley or off duty.

You will be expected to respond to the example set by the crew, and to restrain yourself from using words like 'shit' when encountering areas of turbulence. 'My goodness', 'Dear oh dear', or 'Lord bless us' are okay.

And you must always say 'Thank you' for your plastic TV lunch, and instant coffee, or boiled tea.

It is also permissible to talk to your neighbour about the weather, and to say 'Excuse me' when treading on his or her feet as you go to the toilet.

On leaving an aircraft, you will notice a hostess at the head of the gangway, and another at the foot. They are there to receive your thanks on behalf of their company. So don't say, 'Thank goodness that's over,' or 'Gawd, what a bastard of a ride,' or things like that. Just say, 'Thanks love,' to each of them, and pat them on the shoulder.

Trains: The old coal-burning, stinking, cinder-spitting steam engines are now antiques. (French word.) Australian trains today are pretty good. Trains of the Commonwealth Railways – Sydney to Perth, Port Augusta to Alice Springs – are superb. Quiet, air-conditioned, supremely comfortable, beautifully fitted, they invite casual dress, but etiquette in your behaviour. Pretend you are a 'gentil homme'.

Adopt this pretence also on Inter-City Expresses. Use the ashtrays, drink alcohol from glasses, imbibe soup silently, read serious literature such as *Ladies and Gentlemen*, air your knowledge of wines, and don't spit on the floor.

On all other trains it is good etiket to 'mind your manners'. It is bad etiket to grind your cigarette butts into the floor, spit on it if you need to spit, decorate it with chewing gum wrappers and other unrequired pieces of paper – including your newspaper – smoke in compartments marked 'No Smoking', offer no seats to ladies, and in wet weather to make sure that your umbrella and plastic raincoat drip plenty of water on your neighbour's feet.

You may, however, without fear of giving offence, curse the Government. State Governments own all trains except the 'Indian Pacific' and the 'Ghan', which are owned by the Commonwealth Government. State Government trains, like their buses, incur large annual financial losses.

The motto of the New South Wales Government Railways is 'Orta recens quam pura nites' – recently arisen how pure the light, or something similarly inappropriate. It should be 'Abandon hope all ye who enter here.' The hope will refer to your chances, in Metropolitan areas, of getting a seat in morning or evening peak hours. In country areas it will refer to your chances of getting a pie and coffee at the first stop for refreshments.

The motto of the Queensland Government Railways is alleged to be 'I'll Walk Beside You.' On a train in Queensland once, stopped in the middle of SFA – Sweet Fanny Adams will do for a translation – a visiting traveller asked the guard could he get out and pick some flowers.

'Flowers?' the guard said. 'There are no bloody flowers out here.'

'That's all right,' the traveller said, 'I've got some seeds.'

Work out your own mottoes for other States. Here is a happy traveller's comment for all States:

> 'The Longreach train is late again,
> And things are crook in Tallarook;
> They passed us by in Gundagai,
> There's bugger all in Tocumwal,
> And down in Stawell there's Sweet FA,
> They're out of ale in Lilydale,
> They won't get fatter in Oodnadatta,
> They're buggered up in Manjimup,
> But up in Alice Springs, my friend,
> Get out and walk – it's Journey's End.'

Weddings

You will receive a doubled sheet of white paper with moth-eaten edges, on which will be written:

'Mr and Mrs Stinky Williams request the pleasure of your company at the marriage of their daughter Nausea with Charles Nohoper at St Whatsaname's Church somewhere on Saturday, 21st January, at 3 pm, and afterwards at Mon Repos, such and such a street, somewhere.' And in the bottom right-hand corner will be the letters 'RSVP'.

Bits of paper like this are very formal, very etiquette, very French. In the bottom right-hand corner, the letters 'BWAT' would be better, meaning 'bloody well answer this'. Very etiket. Very Australian. But mothers and daughters do not use or refer to the word 'bloody' in correspondence.

The receiver of the correspondence, however, will probably use the word.

'Bloody hell. Another bloody wedding present. A man'll go bloody broke.'

It will be 'stinkin' hot' on the 21st January, but you will be expected to wear a suit'n tie.

In the church, when you see the groom and his offsider taking their places, you should not call out, 'You'll be sorry.'

And half-an-hour later, when the bride arrives, you should not stand up and let go a wolf whistle.

But you may go to sleep for a while. Somebody will wake you when the show is over, with the words, 'Come on, sport. Don't you want any free grog?'

Free grog will be provided by the bride's father at the reception, and what is called the wedding breakfast, at Mon Repos. It will cost him plenty, but he won't mind. Keeping his daughter costs him more.

At this Mon Repos place, first chance you get make friends with one of the hired waiters. He will then see to it that your glass is never empty. And you can have champagne for breakfast. There is always champagne at wedding breakfasts.

(If you don't like champagne, have a word with your waiter friend. He will find you some beer or Scotch. They keep it 'out the back'.)

After the breakfast, and all the toasts, you may feel like another bit of a sleep. This is not permitted. You must stay until the bride and groom change into their 'going away' togs and have said goodbye to everybody, one at a time.

And you will be expected to dance. The shot here is to go for one of the bridesmaids and 'line her up' for tomorrow, or next week. Bridesmaids are not married. You won't have any trouble with her boy friend. She won't tell him.

Should your moth-eaten invitation show the time of the wedding as something after six o'clock in the evening, you will be expected to wear evening dress.

English and American gentlemen are accustomed to this formal attire. So are some youngish and elderly Australians. But the middle-aged bloke, who hasn't worn his dinner suit for years, has a problem.

His first attempt to solve it, by saying to his wife, 'I'm not goin',' is foiled by her subtle but determined opposition. Women love to go to weddings. And she flatters him by telling him that he looks lovely when he's 'dressed up'.

'I haven't got a dress shirt,' he says.

'Yes you have. I've washed it and ironed it.'

'Oh. Well – what about me cuff links an' studs? I dunno where they are.'

'I do,' she says. 'They're in their little box at the back of the top drawer in the dressing-table.'

'Oh. Well—'

And he digs out his suit. Beauty. He can't wear it. It's covered with mildew. And there's a wine stain, or coffee stain, or something, on the trouser legs.

'I'll take it up to the dry cleaners,' she says.

He can't win. And she's forgotten, or ignored, the fact that since he last wore it he's put on a lot of weight. The shirt collar is too tight. The jacket cramps his shoulders. The waist band of the trousers digs a horizontal hole in his stomach. He complains.

'You look lovely,' she says.

He suffers. The hour in the church feels like a week. There is only one answer. During and after the breakfast he drowns his sorrows and gets stoned.

And spends two weeks in the doghouse because he made an exhibition of himself.

The 'conventional decorum' of European etiquette applies to nearly all Australian weddings. An Australian etiket should be invented.

Suggestion: Casual dress – more of it or less of it according to weather – and a party in the backyard around an eighteen-gallon keg.

Wine Tasting

Some time ago the author of this Bible of correct dress, deportment, and behaviour for all occasions, was invited to a wine tasting at Lindeman's cellars, Marrickville, Sydney.

Wine, food and art expert, Rudy Komon, did the inviting. He rang the morning of the event to check up because he thought the heavy rain that was falling at the time might keep a bloke away. The author's wife answered the 'phone. Rudy told her the function was still on, although, as he said, 'It vas not rainink better; it vas rainink vorse.'

She said, 'I don't think I should let him go. He went to lunch with you and Charlie Moses and Bob Dickerson a few weeks back, to taste some wines, and he arrived home after dark in a shocking condition.'

'Oh but,' Rudy said, 'vine taistink is different. In vine taistink is not drinkink. In vine taistink is spittink out.'

She said, 'If you think that when my old man gets a mouthful of plonk he's going to spit it out, you don't know him very well.'

Very true. Australian wines are too good for 'spittink out'. The best of our wines are as good as, if not better than, anything in the world. And the flagon wines are better than the French 'vin blanc' or 'vin rouge ordinaire'. So, you Poms and Yanks, don't come here yapping about the superior qualities of French, Spanish and Californian wines. They're good, but they are not superior, and therefore are not worth the cost of importation.

And Poms – forget your contention that red wines should be served at room temperature. In your country, except for a couple of days per year, room temperature is, in the words of an anonymous poet of genius,

> 'Cold as an iceberg, gloomy and glum,
> Cold as the hair on a Polar Bear's bum.'

White wine should be served very cold, and red wine at about sixty to sixty-two degrees F – which in England would be a heat wave.

Now in Latin European countries, where wine is the national drink and is even added to the milk in babies' bottles, and where tea and coffee are taxed right out of the worker's pocket, and where beer is a poor imitation of ginger ale, every man is a wine connoisseur. (French word.) He knows, he tells everybody, all about soils and seasons and grape varieties and ageing and blending processes and vintage years, and sniffs and tastes every bottle and gives his verdict.

The sommelier – French for grog waiter – carefully opens a bottle for him, pours a little into his glass and anxiously awaits his verdict.

This is wine etiquette, exported from Europe to the UK, and imported into Australia by our British ancestors. It is 'bulldust'. Like the same imported etiquette that says you should have white wine with white meat, such as chooks, pigeons, galahs, young emus and fish; and red wine with red meat, such as beef, lamb, mutton, buffalo, rabbit and kangaroo.

Aussie etiket, in all aspects of Australian life, counsels you to ignore all 'bulldust'. And even actively to oppose it.

Grog waiters in Australian restaurants strike *their* blow for freedom from 'bulldust' by giving you the wine list before the tucker waiter gives you the menu. The grog waiter doesn't know whether you and your friends are going to order white meat or red. But he stands there, with his little notebook and pencil, waiting for you to look over the string of names and prices – everything the makers and the restaurant owners want to flog – which he's given to you, because you're sitting at the head of the table, and are obviously the host.

Now you forget all these brands, years and vintages. You say to your mob, 'Are yez all havin' plonk?'

One bloke wants beer. You order a bottle for him, and the sommelier writes it down.

'Now, starting from the left, who wants white an' who wants red?'

It always works out about fifty-fifty, so you say to the character with the notebook, 'Give us one of white an' one of red to start with.'

He says, 'Which white would you like, sir? And which red?'

You say, 'I don't give a bugger. None of it's crook, is it?'

He says, 'No, sir. We have a very good cellar. May I suggest a Coonawarra Estate Cabinet-Sauvignon Shiraz, and a Quelltaler Riesling?'

And you say, 'Yeah. Anything you like, mate.'

While he's away, the tucker waiter – or waitress – arrives and starts sliding menus out to everybody as though dealing a hand of 'five hundred'. And after he or she has gone with the orders the grog bloke comes back with the bottle of Van Plonk and the bottle of Red Ned, and goes into his French etiquette act. Which means he will open both bottles, with much flourishing of hands and corkscrew, and pour a little of each into separate glasses, and wait for you to sniff and taste and deliver your verdict.

That's the way he's been trained by his snooty bosses.

But you know, or you should know, that there is no crook Australian wine, and you are not a 'vine taister spittink out', so you stop him and say, 'She'll be right, mate. Send it around.'

And one of your friends is having Quelltaler Riesling with his charcoal grilled steak and spud in foil, and one is having Cabinet-Sauvignon Shiraz Claret with his grilled sole meunière, and another with his fried fillets of john dory and chips.

But who cares? They, and you, have escaped from the wine snobs' 'bulldust', and are having what you want and are therefore happy. And that is all that matters.

Dining Out

Dress

Golf

Afternoon Tea

Loving Thy Neighbour

Christenings

Pie Eating

Correspondence

Speech Making

Fishing